# NO APOCALYPSE

*No Apocalypse*
© 2013 by Monica Wendel

Books published by Georgetown Review Press are available at special discounts for bulk purchases in the United States by corporations, institutions, and other organizations.  For more information, please contact the press at the address listed above.

Book design by Stephen Gullette
Cover photo by Jon Steps

First Edition

ISBN-13:  978-0-615-70598-9
ISBN-10:  0-615-70598-7

Georgetown Review Press
400 East College Street
Box 227
Georgetown, KY  40324

http://georgetownreview.georgetowncollege.edu

# Acknowledgments:

"In Supermarkets in Italy, You Have to Put on Gloves to Touch the Bananas" appeared in *Spoon River Poetry Review*.

"Porn" appeared in *Limestone*.

"Bluestockings Blues" appeared under the title "Poem" in *Forklift, Ohio*.

"Other Islands" appeared under the title "Occupation, Times Square" in *Occupy Writers*.

"'Wikileaks Reveals That Military Contractors Have Not Lost Their Taste for Child Prostitutes'" appeared in *Nimrod*.

"Sexual Assault Awareness Week" appeared in *InDigest*.

"Newton Creek" appeared in *Jellyroll*.

"[The houses off the Palisades Parkway are large and white]" appeared in *Lambda Literary Review*.

"Do you think the Easter Islanders thought there was something else out there?" appeared in *Occupy Writers*.

"Sleeping on a yoga mat in someone else's pajamas" appeared in *Lambda Literary Review*.

"Avon" appeared in *Staccato Fiction*.

"[I fall asleep drunk and dream of Lee Harvey Oswald]" appeared in *Lambda Literary Review*.

"Untitled (Another poem about dreams)" appeared in *Leveler Poetry*.

"Dreams received via text message:" appeared under the title "No Apocalypse" in *InDigest*.

"[Last night a snake rose]" is forthcoming in *Painted Bride Quarterly*.

"Hurricane Poem" appeared in *Pebble Lake Review*.

"Morning through Window" appeared in *H_NGM_N*.

"Epistemology" appeared in *Bellevue Literary Review*.

"Summer" appeared in *Big Bell*.

"Coins" is forthcoming in *Catch-Up*.

"Shannan Gilbert I" is forthcoming in *Midway Journal*.

"Wealth" appeared in *The Brooklyner*.

# Table of Contents

## Politics

## Dreams

## Animals and Cities

## Money and Ghosts

# Political Poems

## In Supermarkets in Italy, You Have to Put on Gloves to Touch the Bananas

I'm not there, though. I'm on the Lower East Side
in a bookstore where a little black dog in a skull & bones
sweater sleeps on a couch, snoring. A bookstore dog.
Whenever I come here I end up rereading the *Redefining Consent*
anarchofeminist zine, but never buy. It starts
with a female-identified female-bodied person
getting sexually assaulted in college, generic story,
so generic that it lacks verisimilitude, but then moves to this weird
personal-responsibility zone with 83 questions
you should ask yourself to find out if you're a rapist.
Number one: have you ever proceeded in a sexual situation
without prior verbal consent? Number two: if verbal
consent was given, did the person's body language or brief moments
of hesitation, intake of breath, quickening pulse,
communicate anything other than consent?
Number three: are you aware of your partner's possible abuse
history as a survivor of sexual assault or as a frat-boy perpetrator
pushing past limits set before punch, Keystone Ice, and close dancing?
It reminds me of the supermarkets in Italy: reaching
for the bananas, my host-sister slapped my hand away
and pointed to the gloves, miming. In my pidgin Italian,
even I understood what she said: how could you have been so stupid?

# For the Birds

At the Hunter protests, no one got arrested except for the crust-punk kids
who started a breaking-stuff dance party right in the middle
of the Communist speaker's speech. It's nice to think
if we destroy capital, we will destroy sexism –
rape being inherently linked to free-market notions of possession –
and if I really believed that, I would have lifted up those trash barrels too
and rolled them into the traffic of 5th Avenue.
Listen hard: money is free speech.
At a party to raise bail for those incarcerated,
a half-dozen anarchofeminists wore armbands
and patrolled the dance floor for safer-space violations.
One of them got so drunk she ended up on the roof, yelling
to a mostly-silent Manhattan skyline: hands cupped to her mouth,
skinny arms jutting out like wings from her face.

# Porn

If you think about it, he kind of always
made money with his body, bike messenger
with thighs of sharp wire, bandana around
his neck to prevent the exhaust of
BQE and Manhattan traffic from going into
his mouth & nose, like a coal miner.
But then his knee got fucked up and I ran into him
at a restaurant we both frequent
and he was talking to an older man about my lawyer
who is kind of a dick but has gotten me
out of a number of situations, and I wouldn't
have gone over to say hi except that
there was this link, a bond
bigger than the house we both lived in or
our weird night bartending a show
for the resisters of somethingmovement –
but the man was not his father, and I slipped
and used the name I knew as his,
and a flash came across his face. I saw
that this is how one lives off of a paper trail,
out of white-collar slavery. It wasn't Jenna Jameson
or *The Da Vinci Co-eds*. This was using
your own thin body for companionship
to a lonely old man. A question of what we own
and what we are willing to sell.

# Bluestockings Blues

Perhaps you are right,
and I have been deceived by drug
companies and scientists
believing that AIDS is real,
believing that vaccines
are not testers for new diseases
that those same companies created
to cure. Sitting in the New School,
your occupation was ready
to bring down the walls of New York City
and from that rubble would emerge
a new world – carried in our hearts –
an anarchist collective without
property, capitalism, evil. Except,
your friend's coat got stolen
at the show we had on Friday night
and since Heather organized it
you want her to pay for the coat,
but Heather says it was your friend's fault
for leaving the coat out in the open
and I want to ask *if neither of you*
*believe in property anyway*
*what's the big deal?* but
the fight multiplies until Heather
moves out. Or is exiled. And the
New School in Exile pushed a few
trash cans into the traffic of 5th Avenue
until the police began putting up fences
but it's clear what's really happening:
this is the beginning of a new world order.

# Other Islands

Here we are, in the great valley of people
between the signs, and the police, and the fences.
Bring me water: I would like that right now.

And the night on the field with the grass and the eels
and the planes rising above us from JFK a dozen miles east –
no one from that night is here.

It feels like I am the only one seeing what I see
and at night I dream of the apocalypse, I am watching the ocean
from above and the tsunami expands like a jellyfish

so perhaps in the dream it actually was a jellyfish,
blue with white edges of waves. The dream-me
checks her cell phone underwater, sends one last text.

In the great mass of people, and then later, walking
down Broadway with police vans stretched for a quarter mile,
I feel very alone; I feel as though no one is watching:

Yet the news ticker lights up again and again
to say where I am, and it is as though I am walking
on the back of a whale, curved slightly, like a parenthesis,
and what I thought was an island indeed was alive.

# A New World In Our Hearts

The radio on always – and Idris left us for Greece –
thin walls suddenly silent.  Sticker downstairs says
I SUPPORT THE BICYCLE BOMBER though

I wasn't in New York for that, now I am, the sly looks
people give me when I tell them *oh I live with Malcolm*
and the Times reports a bicyclist threw a brick
through the window of the Greek embassy.

When a friend's house was tapped in high school,
they took his camera with prom pictures on it so
I only got to look at them after – after what?  I don't know

if he got it back after his brother's trial, or after
his brother was sent away, or if this was something
completely different like the lawsuit still sitting in his room, unsettled.

And unsettling. There are bicycles and bicycles and bicycles
outside my bedroom window.  And like I said, Idris left
for Greece as soon as fighting broke out, I went into
his room for quarters for coffee and saw GREEK

FOR BEGINNERS on the floor although that's something
I think you would take with you, to study on the plane.
Soon after Idris left, Malcolm decided in a big way to stay put,
locked inside the New School in a struggle for longer library hours

and Palestine. He said that this was the city's walls falling.

## "Wikileaks Reveals That Military Contractors Have Not Lost Their Taste For Child Prostitutes"
### headline from www.huffingtonpost.com

Two women say Julian Assange raped them.
Diplomatic cables say contractors in Afghanistan bought boys
for one night or longer. Julian, I can't root for you
while Bradley's alone in the brig. But you're also our best bet.
As for the hackers who took down Visa and MasterCard and PayPal –
I wish it was easier to know what to build.
Like how to make a government without violence,
and which crops besides opium grow in such a harsh climate.
I wish the hackers had found how to reach those boys now,
the ones who danced, veiled, one-named, vague except for this detail:
oldest, age 15; youngest, age 8.

## Sexual Assault Awareness Week

### found poem from jezebel.com

It's our job to carry an umbrella to avoid getting wet
but it's not our job to avoid nighttime, dark streets, and bars
to avoid getting raped. My mother disagrees. An act of man
versus an act of God: what difference does it make, she asks?
Carry your mace and your keys between your fingers,
pointed out like a claw. But what if all the time spent on telling us
what to do differently was spent on telling men, or everyone, not to rape?
The next time I'm told not to take my eyes off my drink
I'm going to print up cards that say, "To avoid perpetrating
sexual assault, be sure not to slip drugs into
anyone's else's drinks." And the next time I'm told that I should always
walk home with a friend, I'm going to hang a checklist that says
you should always walk home with a friend to avoid
sexually assaulting single women. Or single men. A buddy system
is important, or a whistle you can blow if you're afraid
you might rape someone. Think rape whistles blown in bars and
        bedrooms.
The feminist brigade would come running, and the person would say,
*I'm sorry, I'm in this situation where I think I was trying to rape someone.*
*Thank God I had this whistle and you came.*

# Newton Creek (Brooklyn/Queens Border)

Newton Creek, wider than the Genesee River,
half-canal anyway, old dumping ground for sewage
and the scum left after refining ore.
We are balancing, cannot hold hands.
He shifts from concrete block to concrete block
sneakers steady, as though he is on the jetty
by his mother's house, rocks and skin
covered with the thin layer of salt brought by the Sound.
Two days after he broke his jaw,
he shared his painkillers and we floated,
our feet the same level as the water,
moving like the air itself was water. When I dreamt,
his dream-him had his jaw wired shut too, and in my dream
he could not open his mouth to kiss me.
Now each street turns into dead-ends,
signs read "Guards Armed and Unarmed,"
"Beware of Dogs." The streets are lined with too-nice cars
that don't fit in, that may or may not be mob cars
because there is always a government in place,
especially the places where government has left.
Like the way a tide recedes and leaves behind
detritus: the garbage, yes, but also the creek itself,
oozing slowly, unused locks for ships with nowhere to go.

# [The houses off the Palisades Parkway are large and white]

as birthday cakes. Rick Santorum mourns the lost
ghost ship of his child, its body returned to outside air,
the air of the living, air of his ambition. He has lost
and now all women must pay for this death.
It is our wombs that harbored and then rejected life.
I hear his voice on the radio when I'm driving,
looking at those fucking houses, their monstrous
footprints. Even as far north as here the Hudson
is not a *river* river moving from St. Lawrence to
New York Bay but is a *tidal* river that moves in,
and out, and in again, in accordance with the moon.
Sweater-vest Santorum knows he'll never win
my state, but grief continues to propel him forwards.
Every drug-store condom is a reminder to him
of the child that never was; the government
ought to take those things away. Child. Child. House.
Dead child. Its weight in his arms. Its weight
in his children's arms. The voices of the dead
sailing past me on the river. The river that I
have not stepped in yet. A grief I refuse to enter.

# September, Red Hook

We cut bread into thick chunks and knelt by the edge of the canal. Like white footsteps, they bobbed unevenly in the water for a moment, then started moving towards the bay, pushed by an unseen wind. "Dinner for seagulls," you said. "Or a raft for a mouse who's getting tired of swimming."

The sky was clear. We made our way home between old factories. Inside, Mother was washing panties in the sink and stringing them up around the kitchen with twine. It smelled like wood. We took the ladder to the roof, winced as our palms touched its dark tar. In the distance, the elevated train pulled its passengers closer to home. I could see the geometric shape of its tracks and support beams.

But it was you who spotted our bread first. "Look. There." The oil slick from the canal had dyed the white bread and we could make out each piece against the dark water of the bay. Mine was an ice cream sunset of purple and gold. Yours was the green of the park and the pale pink of Mother's lips.

We sat with our legs dangling over the side of the building, watching the bread drift like glass beads sliding down a giant's belly, towards the smoldering towers of Lower Manhattan. "Maybe a firefighter will eat it," I said, "as a snack." You lifted your head towards the seagulls and said nothing. "Or maybe," I said, "it's a landing raft for someone in the ashes who jumped."

## Do you think the Easter Islanders thought there was something else out there?

When the sun sets, early, before Halloween,
we are standing in the park with the river to one side
and the buildings tall beyond the river.
It feels like being within a small circle, sun leaving.
It feels like we are leaving.
When Leela asks that, about the Easter Islanders,
I don't know if she's saying, look – even those people
weren't stupid enough to think what we're thinking, even they
knew that beyond everything they'd ever seen
there's more. Or if she was saying the opposite:
that we are just like them, on an island,
and we know just as little as they knew. Or if maybe
she was saying something completely different
about environmental destruction and the collapse of a civilization
but right around when I reach that last theory
the sun slips away behind Manhattan
and the Freedom Tower's lights turn on
and we start talking about Occupy Wall Street,
their colonies like spores, in the Privately Owned Public Spaces
which are also like islands, or volcanoes,
the atria and lobbies of financial buildings
that were built past regulation, past building code.
And then once we start talking about that
I think about what it means to put out a fire
and what it means for a building to burn with men in it
and the sun setting over the river looks like that fire.

# Howl-ish

The same night Hobart passed out in the Centre Street Station
Malcolm passed him on his way to the train, but said
nothing. And that was the night that Leela told Seth
she had a crush on us – she didn't say it was us,
but she hinted, and then two weeks later
we all hooked up in Megan's bed with the clean sheets and tall
window over an empty lot. I'm nostalgic for that
makeshift family, the houses without doors, Leela's grey boy-
short underwear with a seam straight down the center, my breath
on it, life easier than I'd ever known it. I guess I know how
these things fall apart. There was unpaid rent and jealousy
and Adderall and the windows broken at the 1 2 3 Space
after they got evicted, that last party that I refused to go to and Seth said
people danced in broken glass and spilled paint,
Leela with a backpack full of drugs and her shirt unbuttoned
with another girl's hand down it. A lot died with that space.
Dave Solidarity's bike accident settlement money and an after school
program and hot food for Saturday afternoons in Von King Park.
I mean, how do you let it all go?
And it is enough just to name what you love?

## While the sky changes over the crowd on Wall Street

The bitter taste of arugula in my mouth –
flies gather on the ceiling above us.

I pretended to be someone else
so you could love me without guilt.

Remember your brother's blood in the sink,
the bathroom fouled?

That night, the first time you washed my clothes with your own.

# Dreams

# Willoughby Street

One kind of bird for the round nut.
Another for the oval. Florence in my dream
was tan and pink; we drank Coronas on a roof
and passed around a pipe, its smoke clear
but present. My old house wasn't cold enough
for me to see my breath in, but it was too cold
for cockroaches. The mice cried at night,
ran during the day to stay warm.
One, scared, skirted around my foot when I ate lunch.
Malcolm brought in the cat then, and the beast delivered
seven corpses lined up before my door, flawless
save for blood in their tiny mouths & ears.

# I am sleeping on a yoga mat in someone else's pajamas

A Christmas tree in the courtyard below turns the bedroom walls pink. The lamp on the ceiling is a cloud. In the dream there is a book of sonnets in my hands, with a cover of thick leather. You gave it to me. We are drinking in the dark and staying sober. You sit down and I stand and your ex-girlfriend, the one who I've never met, appears. Neither of us knows what we are supposed to know about the other, but she is kind. A cat runs across the room, chasing a dark mouse. When I wake up, a trapeze artist is wrapped up next to me in a white comforter, sitting up, her face as pointed and bright as a Hershey's kiss. Outside a gypsy cab honks, looking for passengers.

# Secrets, Or: Why I Can't Prove That There Is Not An Invisible Cat In That Empty Chair[9]

Sometimes I feel like the only person
who doesn't believe that 9-11 was an inside job.
Maybe the absence of 9-11 files from Wikileaks
proves something, although in college I thought a lot
about how the absence of proof for God does not mean
that God is absent. I've clearly been reading
too much Wikileaks if I'm thinking this much about God.
Last night I dreamt I was in an Israeli prison
and none of my friends knew where I was.
I couldn't convince the guards that I was really Jewish.

All this reminds me of City College, up in Harlem,
where my grandfather went when Harvard's Jew quota was filled.
My boyfriend still tells me that Israeli workers were warned
not to go to work at the World Trade Center that day,
and again I find myself arguing against the existence of something
whose nonexistence cannot be proven.

---

9       C.S. Lewis: "We are arguing like a man who should say, if there were an invisible cat in that empty chair, the chair would look empty; but the chair does look empty; therefore there is an invisible cat in it."

# Avon

Dinner.
I am drunk on white wine, arguing with my Greek metaphysics professors three times my age on matters of immigration and he pulls out pictures of his children from his wallet. One of them is named Sophia.

Around seven, the wife calls the house while we are eating. I go home and have sex twice with myself and fall asleep without dreams.

Later.
I know nothing will change the matter of the house and empty rooms, the white shag carpet in the living room and the glass table above it and the big windows I can see stars out of and in my mind I see myself lying down on the carpet and touching the threads between my fingers to not be dizzy and not be worried about if my face is read and if my pro-immigration argument makes sense and on the long drive home through back woods past farms and farmhouses a la *Texas Chainsaw Massacre* I realize I barely ate and barely said anything of any meaning and would like to turn the car back and cook again maybe bake brownies fill up the house so it is loud with us.

Questions.
How much longer will we be here? Any of us. I mean also my dog and my brother's three goldfish and my brother who turned 17 on Saturday. Of course the soup we made had chicken broth in it so all I could think of when I was trying to eat was dear old Franny's cup of consecrated chicken soup, holy chicken soup and it went cold when I was thinking about its holy holy holiness.

More Questions.
He wanted to know if David Leckford ever propositioned me in office hours, or invited me to his house to exercise in his gym or meditate on his pillows, and I thought, is that what he sees in me? Am I the type of student who gets propositioned during office hours in Welles 114 while I'm trying to write a paper on the Buddha?

The whole thing made me feel small. Like my hands and feet were creatures trying to find their way through the earth.

# [I fall asleep drunk and dream of Lee Harvey Oswald]

I fall asleep drunk and dream of Lee Harvey Oswald –
in the dream, I'm his wife, the one he beats,
and we have a baby who knows how to open doors.
He's not faithful. He has sex with a schoolteacher on the front seats
of our car, and when she gets out, it's raining. The rain
is a sheet over the front steps, puddles on the walkway,
but something pink or red floats on top. Petals?
He's going to kill her and I wake up. When I remember the dream
I wonder if someone I'm having sex with is going to kill me.
I remember sitting at the window in the apartment in Baltimore
icing my wrist and face and how guilty it felt,
that I hadn't made it work. The summer of cicadas.
Their bodies three deep. I can't tell if I'm still that woman.
I can't tell if it's going to happen again.

# Four Short Poems About Dreams

In the early morning, waking, I dream that my brother is still in the hospital. We are waiting. We are watching a movie. Then I am in the movie, under dark blue water, swimming towards a wall that is painted like the sky. What movie is this? I can see an old lover on the dock, shotgun in hand, waiting for me to surface.

*

I wake in the middle of the night, 4 am, dreaming that my brother is still in the hospital. I need to get there. My friends are sitting in a circle. One of them looks up and starts talking to me about finding an apartment. I need a car. I need to get to the hospital. I wake up.

*

This time I am not dreaming. I am at a wedding outside of Albany. There are peacocks wandering the grounds. My old lover, the one from the dream, is there. During dinner I step out and call my brother. I am too drunk to speak. I look at the number on my phone for a long time.

*

Sunlight white as an atom bomb's blast, it is the days that are the hardest.

# Untitled (Another poem about dreams)

My belly is a liquid sac and my teeth
have turned to coins. I am waiting

for you at the end of a long hallway with only
one small window. Every day we drag the bench

from one place to another and every day they drag it back.

It is not enough to say "I want" –
you are bigger than wanting. I have never
loved so much and done so little.

# Dreams received via text message:

"Did we ever drive in a forest at night and then fight our way through an abandoned church? Did I already describe this happening in a dream? I think I saw a ghost last nite."

"Are you sure? Never like a church full of bushes and mannequins? While we were sort of being menaced by maniacs? I feel like we did this at some point."

"No apocalypse – just desolate and a scene urging escape. Long winding forest road dimly lit and then a grotto in an overgrown but not abandoned church lobby. Then I woke up and think I saw a ghost with a beard and a malevolent look."

"You could come get in bed too! – I thought that was very exciting last time. (Don't think I'm supposed to say this – feeling a bit priapic this morning). Yeah sleeping late – both symptom and cause of depression."

"Come over and I'll make us coffee here while getting up? I'm just waking up."

# Re: Dhalamshala

*That sounds terrible -- quiet, empty mornings,*
*as the street starts to get hot, feel right, but the nightmare –*
*I grind my teeth, but never know*
*what for, never remember my nightmares.*

*

The hottest in New York in decades.
Drinking and blue pills for the sunrise.
This is why I am dreaming, in the daylight,
of a cock or a gun. Sometimes I have one
and sometimes I have the other.

*

*Do you remember how we met? because I don't*
*remember how we met. I am not good*
*at remembering beginnings of certain things.*

*

We saw a ship far-off in the sea
waiting to enter New York Harbor.
And the land under our feet
had been washed over, by the hurricane,
had been sifted in an earthquake.

*

*If you are coming there, I will be there at that time there also.*

*

If I took off a fingernail, and you gave me the wings in return,
how many turns before we exchanged selves?
I remember how we met. Remember Panama?
The canal turned the tops of mountains into islands.
Today I stood on the shore for a long time
and wrote this, to you.

# I dream that I am being forgiven.

He saw me by the big metal gates of Bellevue Hospital
and then I took him and his friend for sandwiches.
We watched the sun set over those buildings
while he named the people watching him and I interrupted
to find out the names of the parks where he slept at night.
His friend listened and told me that the hospital
gives sandwiches, and toothbrushes.
How strange that I had just been inside,
writing memos, while they were outside on the lawn.
We tried to count how many times
we had each walked past each other
or above and below each other.
And now when I walk through those parks
I am watching for friends who I have not seen for too long a time.

# Study of Brick, Baltimore

arm over flame     gas stove     how to write
of betrayal     or know it     eyes rimmed always
   as if with black rope     no it is eyeliner   no
it is charcoal     the sign of a cross in ash     it is ash
   the wind sifts it     as though it is breathing
     it speaks     Baltimore row houses     jagged close
as teeth     branches tangle     clink against glass against
     each other     never quite connecting
a sink clogged     vomit     half-digested almonds
     clean sheets on the bed     bike's chain grease on the floor
her eyes still     unapologetically large     bangs slanted
   over them     my mouth on hers     a dark well
skin patched with burns     her own

# [Last night I dreamt that a snake rose]

Last night I dreamt that a snake rose
from the bedside table, knocked against the window
with his nose until I opened it. The rain woke me,
rain thawing the ice on the sidewalk, my hands
slow and thick as honey on the window ledge.
Freud would say my teeth felt strange.
Freud would say the snake was my guilt,
trying to leave, unable to do so secretly.
But I tried to let it out, I start arguing with Freud,
lying on my back and imagining. Didn't you see?
I opened the window and now my hands are dirty.
Then I am awake in the real world. I am arguing
against a past that was real once, but not anymore.

# Re: Rain today

Last night, we fell asleep to the sound of traffic.
I woke early, when it was still dark,
and watched the stoplight outside change from red to green
and back. I wanted to go inside of you.
I wanted to see what your dreams were.
Of course, I fell back asleep and in the afternoon
high winds knocked a billboard off the expressway.
It smashed into a building but no one was hurt.
From the street it looked like a futuristic shelter,
with thick metal tubes almost like plumbing.
Unless I was looking at it wrong. In the cold,
waiting for something to change,
the cars avoided the expressway, the news cameras set up
and took down, and the firemen and police officers went
about their business, rosy-cheeked, dead-eyed.
Were you in your office? Were you at your apartment?
Were you still where I had left you – in bed, thin limbs
sprawled under the blankets that I had kicked off, sweating?
I hope you slept after I left, and not fitfully.
All of today felt far beyond those early-morning hours.

# Animals and Cities

# Great White Sails

the grass is kept
      indefinitely adolescent
mowing the tops off
      it grows sideways

we lie on our backs
      bellies to the sun
waves furl and unfurl
      great white sails

## "Man holding another man's head"

And the great abandoned building arched up and rounded
like a whale rising through water for air –
I did not think, oh, we have killed so many
of your kind – I thought instead of the planes
rising from behind the ocean, from Europe, from Asia,
to us, to New York, our canals and shores and people
and I lay down on the concrete and saw a face
and peacock eyes in the leaves and stones
until it wore off, and I was ill, but still mystified,
my sick belly heavy.
Between the tents was our cove and from there the tents
rose like walls – I nested –
wondered about the dolphins which still mate
mere miles from the runway – my teeth felt weak as baleen –
and I lay still and let it be morning,
until it was.

## Hurricane Poem

By the time the storm arrives,
the soil will already be saturated.
I wish there were a part of me
that didn't hurt. In my first real storm
the rain fell to my beer; I had no covering.
There is no more us. When will the worms
return to their canyons? What pills are these
beneath the carpet? I am eating
food that grows in the dark. I am washing
my hands and watching the sky.

# 178th Street Port Authority Bus Terminal

A pigeon thumps against scuffed walls
but his mates are content on the floor.
They gather around discarded Chinese food

takeout, and I shudder at the ignominy
of a pigeon eating pig. Trying my damndest
to avoid touching doorknobs, arm-rests, I am

tired and growing sick, or perhaps sick
and therefore tired. Hand sanitizer and gel
flow like a river that no one steps in twice.

A man in baggy clothes and without shoelaces
scratches his back on the bench, rocking.
It is cold out, high of 38, if the snow

does come it will pile like blown tissues.
If a man lives in a bus station, is he homeless?
Bathrooms, heat, lights, restaurants downstairs.

Up the stairs, my bus pulls in. Finally we move
over the bridge, sky a grey syrup. I'm not
the only one watching the clouds thicken;

in the distance, men emerge from beneath
the bridge, carrying their belongings, moving,
like me, towards shelter.

# Reconstruction

Piece by piece the walls fall. Sheltered behind paintings
and pictures a hidden world of mouse poop, quarters.
The colors of memory: flesh tones and grass.
White numbers you wore on your back, sweat soaking through.

We say we will put it back together
after all the dirt is cleaned out. We dream of walls
painted blue, mold dried out to dust.
Punch a hole through the house and we will call it a window.
Call it a window and we will sleep under the stars.

# Morning through Window

Outside our window, men walk by with limbs in their arms.
They are chopping down the hemlock trees while inside
we lie in bed, lentils simmering on the stove.
It is September. The sky ripples, and I reach my arm out to you.

To test airplanes for cracks, workers send sounds across them.
Other mornings, in the darkness of semi-sleep, I listened to the train
as it moved towards the city, and pictured my father stepping onto it,
reading the paper or dozing as it traveled under a river, surfacing in
      Midtown.

I want to say we belong in water, not in air. Even in the weeks
when the smoke settled over the river, we still counted the rats
on the 7 train's tracks, gave them names, pictured them as commuters.
Down by Rockaway Beach stray cats do battle in the marshland near the
      runway
where the great metal bellies of planes lower themselves from the sky.

# Liberation Theology

My friend brings me stolen gifts –
cookies from Whole Foods,
American Apparel leggings.

No cat or dog growing up,
but he had a rooster rescued
from a fighting ring, a life

of amphetamines and razorblades.
Bloodbeak would scream from the garage,
peck at its own flesh if you

came near. And somewhere outside
activists don black balaclavas
to perform rescue operations

on pit pull puppies, roosters,
sweatshop sewn sneakers. We eat
standing up in the cold kitchen.

# Epistemology

I dream of water, and pools, standing on my tiptoes
and tilting my chin up to break the surface. I know
I'm supposed to love rivers, but I don't. I only love
great open expanses that throw up carcasses before us
as offerings or sacrifices.

Tuesday evenings we drop off bread at the Grove –
bags of it, drops condensing inside the plastic
when it has been sealed still steaming.
No matter how many times we go,
they must look at us first through the two-way mirror.

His family moves around the house like
chess pieces: a limping knight, a slow, almost-
crippled king, the queen appearing where
one least expects her. And no board but the sound of the TV.

Horseshoe crab, I will never know your suffering.
Ancient body, ancient shell. What have we done
by lying next to you, unknowingly, and making love?

# Pope John Paul II Square

I keep rediscovering my old grocery lists.
There are fresh strawberries at the farmer's market – who knew?
And when the Virgin falls from her pedestal on the corner
the groundskeeper straightens her within hours.
In Brooklyn, I've also learned that the nuns
frequent the pizza place over the Polish diner,
and that their habits are brown, not black, with white edges.
In the mornings, in grey light on a grey street,
we nod to each other on the way to the bus stop.

# From the Shore

From the shore, one can see cars crossing the bridge,
and the subway pulling the long rope of itself,
but walkers and bikers are too small to make out.
I thought about the whores in Shakespeare's plays –
how they provide companionship, like a girlfriend would.
I thought about it since I have a boyfriend, but I don't love him,
and I also have a lover, but I'm not sure I like him.
My boyfriend and I meet on the street
while my lover and I meet in cool, dark rooms
four or five floors up to undress each other with precision.
I wish I could be the same in all of these places,
a singular self propelled forward – but I am like a river
that forks around land, becomes smaller or larger or more salty,
and then reunites, on the other side, with itself.

# Questions

Of course plants grow from between rocks and in sidewalk cracks.
Where else would a helicopter be but overhead?
I've always loved biospheres and bubbles – dish soap, not gum.
My students love imagining animals together
to make newer, crazier animals, like anaconda alligators
that teach the class how to break dance.
Sometimes when I leave, they know what a story is.
Sometimes when I leave I feel the cool water off the canal
and wonder why we try to build rivers where there are none.
Whose fault is it, really, if it becomes polluted,
bubbling and aflame? Think of volcanoes.
Think of birds nesting with bits of yarn.
Of course all we long for is home.

# Library

The other day, we made love on the living room couch under a grey sky. I hate the phrase "make love" but sometimes I can't think of any better words. Your throat was raw with strep and so we didn't talk, or rather, you didn't talk, miming with your hands where you wanted my tongue to go. When we both read <u>Wind-Up Bird Chronicles</u> sex got even better. It was spring and rainy and in the book, the narrator keeps going into wells and falling asleep and having wet dreams and it was like we were role playing a lost man, a disappeared cat, a bird that foretells death. But I'm not sure which one I was, and which one you were.

# Summer

On Tuesday afternoon, the rain rising from the sidewalk
carried with it little dog-poop particles. It's amazing
the jobs you never tell your parents you work – artist's model,
shot girl, babysitter of rich wives. I hate being asked what I desire.
Sometimes it feel like there's a cord from my knees to my sternum
that gets plucked when our knees touch. But sometimes not.
I almost always date vegetarians, and my cheap cell phone
distorts voices too much for long, meaningful conversations.
I'm tired of talking in cars while the world blurs
outside plastic windows. My problem is that I used to fuck
like I was in love when I really wasn't, and now I don't know how
to fuck at all anymore. I want you to look at me. I've a vegan
who sneaks banana bread without asking the ingredients
and who doesn't stop the waiter who adds baba ghanoush to my falafel.
I want to say I've already done my part, but that's never true.
Do you know of the stroke victim who writes poems with her toe?
She always starts with the first letter, and turns her head from side to side
like a runner's arms pumping through air. Now I've sobered up.
Now I'm waiting for a phone call from someone who I hurt.

# [Spring is a falling backwards.]

Spring is a falling backwards.
When I close my eyes I see dead bees
or the glistening, spotted backs of slugs.
Lust is my greatest sin, but never with you.
In the lobby he circled his arm around my waist.
Left for work and I lay on my back and listened.
Someone turned on the shower next door.
Traffic moved five stories below.
I floated. I remembered.

# An Aquarium

Headache. I touch myself until it fades
but then it's back 10, 15 minutes later.
Wash my hands in the sink – blood on them,
my period's not over yet – no roommates home
to witness the Macbeth moment.
The problem with the world today
is that people keep having children.
If they just stopped breeding there would be no more tragedies.
Besides, it's often better on your own
in your own room or on your own bed
with no one to apologize to for being too loud
or not being loud enough. I hate sex as a team sport
or a corporate project where everyone
has to put in their all. Sometimes it's like
I come from a foreign country
where the only person who speaks the language
is myself, where the only other living creatures
are silent, floating animals –
jellyfish on sand or riding the crests of waves.

# Love @ Hotel Q

Time in Times Square. Or no time at all in us.
No clocks in pools.
No clocks in bars.
No clocks in pool bars.
No clock at the bottom of my drink.
His name – said – and then he existed before me –
me saying it made it so. Under heat and skin
there he was, through steam, through water.

His hair, dark and curly.
I remember candles lit outside
and the bugs that move away from the candles outside.
His hand is too big, knuckles moved wrong
as they healed.

My hand, unbroken. Hair, wet again.
Chlorine sticks to my hair. My hair sticks to itself.
There's love wriggling away somewhere. It's smooth.
It feels like mucus, runs quicker than subway rats.

Counting rats on the subway, warm white air.
Rat. Rat. Rat. Fall on the tracks?
Duck and crouch. Rat. Rat.
15 minutes 'til the L train. 12 minutes.
Clock slides down. Train slides in.

# Jacksonville

A fly stamps its feet on my skin. Tiny terrorist,
or rapist, its proboscis cuts through me
to draw blood. I hit it; they are slow
when they are sated, and its tiny squashed body,
legs only as wide as my arm hair,
releases my own blood. Meanwhile the air conditioner
expels warm air into the backyard. Perhaps
the insects like it better. Down in Florida,
a power plant releases warm water into the swamps
and manatees are drawn to the great grey Leviathan;
like a perverted Jonah, they wait at a city's mouth
to be swallowed by what we exhale.

# Autobiography, 1999

If I stare hard enough at the leaves on the tree outside his window
eventually he will turn to look and see what is there.  He has

horn-rimmed glasses, too skinny.  I say, I have more cuts on my arm,
I didn't tell you about them before.

He looks and says "oh they're deep"
He says "you have deep-rooted feelings of guilt"

so I tell him about the dream. I was harvesting babies
for their organs in my backyard.  I was up

to my forearms in dark blood before I woke up
and also, Kyle Brown dumped me.

I knew I was going crazy. It was just a matter of how crazy?
Not very. Just little wisps firing off inside. I felt like my mind

had been split open and put back together all jumbled up.
Nothing matched right, I heard my name

called over and over again and then the bathroom
became an office became people outside. I barricaded

myself in. Then I woke up my parents.
That was when Kyle still liked me, though. I felt

like a cat – slender, taut, rubbing myself against him.
Once his father opened the door, stood there

in his underwear, white undershirt, white boxer/briefs.
He seemed to float there – I was floating there –

it was 4 am – Kyle and I didn't dare breathe.
I could have picked up the marshmallow street lights

plucked them one by one, a white picket fence around us.
Kyle's forehead had a scar from the time

his father pushed his head through a wall. In my town
people like Kyle's father didn't exist. There were

fathers like mine who drank until they blacked out
and my mom had to drive us to piano lessons and the doctor's

but no one ever hit their kids. Eventually
he closed the door and it was like

no sound had ever been made at all.
I was on top of Kyle, his hands on my sides

and when the door closed was also when the heat
of Kyle's body hit me, it was like a furnace,

it was his hands and his cock and his legs,
all of it seemed hot enough to hurt.

He never walked me home, but he did
read my poetry, tuck my hair behind my ear,

tell me I was the most beautiful girl in school.
And I felt better about the dumping

after he started doing e, dropped out of school,
moved to Oregon – although as my revenge

I kissed his brother during an Andy Goldsworthy movie
at Huntington's Cinema Arts Centre and his brother

made me a necklace to correspond with my heart charka
and it was only after that that I told him I didn't like him,

never really had. I was 17 by then, it was
three years after Kyle, and Kyle didn't care at all –

in this new life he was back from Oregon, had grown
his hair long, given up cigarettes, didn't speak to

his father anymore. When I remember
what it was like being fourteen, I remember that

I had always wanted to touch his father's face that night –
lead him, glowing, to the window

where the streetlamps breathed before us. He saw
me by their glow, the curves of my hips and legs –

a body taking shape under someone else's hands.

# Money and Ghosts

# Ghosts, Memory, Grief

Above, the stars reach out their arms –
I see guns in the sky, headlights of a car
driven through the rain – a rocket,
falling, red, arcing like a mouth through
the sky – which is now turning purple,
Batman-movie purple, and an anarchist boy
with his black hood up and black bandana over
his mouth leaps now, over the barricades, removes
one, I recognize him from his eyes, the only
part of him that is visible, the eyes I knew
when he slept out on the roof after a party
when none of us felt like cleaning – and he
is motioning now, for us to come through,
and we do, and the face of Trayvon Martin
comes too, it is printed in color on signs
and the text below his smile says
protect our children, and with that, already,
he has ceased to be a real boy
and he is now the ghost we are carrying
through the streets like a coffin draped
in a flag, or something less heavy,
less corporeal. An officer in a white shirt
grabs my arm and I twist out and away
and pull my hood up too in the crowd
it is more like we are the sea and his body
is floating on us, not weighing us down,
we exist to hold him because we are
no graveyard, we are a place for the not-real,
for the things that once existed and exist
no more, a child next to me climbs up
on her father's shoulder and I wonder
what she can see from there, within
the bodies there is no sense of scale, only that
we fill the streets curb to curb, only
that we are heading south to Zucchotti
Park as though there will be something
when we get there, and when we get there
there are only cops guarding the
empty park its bare benches and concrete floor
and would could be there besides
memory, anyway.

# Coins

There is salt on my hair and on my skin.
In late afternoon I eat, finally, cold food
from the fridge, bubbling soda can.
We make a play. We touch ourselves.
I am never alone. When will you learn
to accept things as they are?
I am talking to myself again.
I am telling stories in which I save you.

# Mexico City

I leave you in New York and you email me about 9/11.
No plane crashed into the Pentagon. The flight
over Pennsylvania ended when passengers were brought
to a secret Midwestern concentration camp and executed.
You know because you've thought a lot about it. I read
the letters on my Blackberry, interrupted by text messages
and a waiter refilling my drink. You miss me like this?
Like a missing airplane? Like dead bodies? Do you know
your stories aren't real? When I wake in the morning I look
out over Mexico City, clear before the pink smog begins to gather.
The money here is pink too, like Monopoly money,
but it's real because we believe that it's real.
Even you believe that. I return when it is your face
that I start to see in the clouds.

# Traditions

My boyfriend and I always have sex
on the first day of my period, and never use a condom.
Sometimes I forget that the blood
is my period, and, when he pulls out,
another tide pulls my chest under
and tells me that this is the first time,
something has changed or broken.
This is not really the case, and jars
my memory when I sell my underwear
at a love motel, *no touching*, for $75.
Even stranger when all I do with that money
is go to the mall and buy more underwear.
My boyfriend likes it. He likes the new cotton
under his hands, or a strap that rises up
when I sit down, and he likes when I tell him
the story of the turnpike and the motel,
the man's shaven head and when he dropped
hints about a wife ... *just traveling through*,
the man said, as though I was worried
that I might see him again.

## Shannan Gilbert I

I know what it's like to travel through a salt marsh,
mud that sucks the boots, then the socks, from your feet
until it is your bare flesh in the mud
and your legs are too tired to tear them out.
Is that when the tide approached?
You could see, a mile or so away,
the lights from the causeway, but how
could you know what lay in between?

It took a year to find your body, less than a mile
from the gated community. First they had to drain the water
and ride over what was left – the flat, salty land.

## Shannan Gilbert II

Shannan, they looked for you and found the others
and the others were divided, man and women,
child and adult, hands thirty miles east from a body –
so the police divided and divided again, there were two men
at work, plus a third who wanted to get rid of a child,
three killers overlapping graveyards and shifts,
but now that they have found you they are combining
theories, it is only one person, perhaps a fisherman
with a pickup truck and early-morning beach access,
perhaps a cop with untraceable cell phone, perhaps a John Doe
infamous in circles, whispered, *don't go to him.*
Your body became a map, untraceable, untouchable in death.
They could not put a hand on you. It sounded a bell
and they looked in the bushes and found all of those
who were not you. Scrub brush, beach plums, mussels.
The marsh emptying into the ocean in salty arrows.

## Shannon Gilbert III

You found him, on a message board full of "straight men"
looking for "another straight man" to "suck my cock."
If you had been that, would you have survived? How many
roses did he offer, how many did you ask for, was travel
included? Looking on Craigslist, the picture that you used
makes you seem so tiny. But you weren't. I want to lift you
from the marshland, the way Neanderthals were mummified
in bogs, features intact, and say look, you showed us
where the others were. That is the opposite of small.
What about a woman causes that in a man?
(And now, alone, I wish so much that you were still alive.)

## Wealth

The bitten lip of the moon spills over the clouds.

Every beer is drunk down. Every blackout ends with morning.

When I do bad things, I want to brag about them. I want you to know
how far I went.

What wealth the tide leaves behind, only to take it again.